# MICHAEL LAWSON

To the memory of
Barbara Lawson (1910–1993) and
C.W.E. Lawson (1903–1979)

*Untitled*, 1967
Enamel on Masonite, 61⅞ by 49⅛ in.
Whatcom Museum of History and Art,
Bellingham, Washington, gift of
Mr. and Mrs. C. Bagley Wright, Seattle

By Matthew Kangas

PORTLAND PRESS
Seattle

## Acknowledgments

This project began as early as 1986, when I first curated a mini-survey of Michael Lawson's art at Bumbershoot, Seattle's annual arts festival, and realized that a much more thorough survey was long overdue. Since then, with the encouragement and support of John Olbrantz, deputy director of the Whatcom Museum of History and Art, and Dale Chihuly, Lawson's close friend and the one responsible for his coming to Seattle in the first place, the exhibition and this document have come to fruition. Many people are due thanks besides John and Dale, including all the collectors and artists who graciously lent works, and many others who spoke with me, remembered Seattle in the heyday of the 1960s, and shared information and thoughts with me about Lawson and his incalculable impact on figurative painting in Seattle during and shortly after those years. I am grateful also to Michael Jacobsen for his thoughtful installation of the exhibition; to Cathy Westfeldt, Whatcom Museum registrar; to Gale Joice, interim director, Seattle Art Museum, for the generous loan; to Diane Douglas and Susan Sagawa of the Bellevue Art Museum; to the photographers who worked hard and fast to meet deadlines; to the catalog designer Karen Johnson for her beautiful work; to Barry Rosen and Rob Millis of Portland Press; to Margaret Sarsfield and Dave Marshall of Liverpool for their hospitality during my 1989 visit; and to Michael Lawson for his enthusiastic support and unending patience over a long period. Without him, none of this would have been possible.

**Matthew Kangas**
*Guest Curator*


Published on the occasion of an exhibition held at the Whatcom Museum of History and Art, Bellingham, Washington, from October 23, 1993, to January 16, 1994.





Designed by Karen Johnson, Level 29 Design
Distributed by University of Washington Press, Seattle and London
ISBN-0-9608382-4-4
Printed in the United States of America

Portland Press
P. O. Box 45010
Seattle, Washington 98145-0010

**Contents**

*A Park in a Room*, 1966
Enamel on Masonite, 68 by 48 in.
Seattle Art Museum,
Eugene Fuller Memorial Collection, 68.204
PHOTO: PAUL MACAPIA

# Foreword

Born in Liverpool, England, in 1944, Michael Lawson was educated at the Liverpool College of Art and the Royal College of Art in London. He moved to the United States in the mid-1960s to study at the University of Wisconsin and the University of Washington. It was in Seattle in the late 1960s that Lawson began to develop his mature style.

When Lawson arrived in Seattle in the late 1960s, the local art scene was dominated by abstract art. Lawson's evolving figurative style, with its emphasis on bright colors and strong narrative content, would have a profound influence on a number of local artists, including Fay Jones and Gene Gentry McMahon; in effect, it helped validate their own figurative impulse, which would reach maturity in the early 1980s.

"Michael Lawson: The Seattle Years" attempts to examine the work of this highly regarded English painter within the context of contemporary regional art. Although he has not lived in Seattle since the early 1970s, his impact on contemporary Seattle art has nevertheless been significant and profound.

On behalf of the Board of Trustees and staff of the Whatcom Museum of History and Art, I would like to thank a number of people without whose help this exhibition and publication would not have been possible.

I would like to express my thanks and appreciation to Dale Chihuly who, together with Matthew Kangas, first suggested the idea of a Michael Lawson exhibition to me. Chihuly, an old friend of Lawson's from the University of Wisconsin, has kept in close touch with the painter over the years, has acquired a number of drawings and paintings in the past, and has generously agreed to underwrite the cost of the exhibition catalogue.

I am further indebted to Matthew Kangas, a Seattle-based art critic and curator, for his selection of objects in the exhibition and his insightful essay. As always, Karen Johnson has designed a publication that stands as a beautiful tribute to the artist and his work.

A project of this scope would not have been possible without the full support of a number of lenders and contributors, and to them I am most grateful. While I cannot thank each of them personally, their names appear in other parts of this book.

Finally, and by no means least, I would like to thank Michael Lawson for his time and help with the project. When the art history of our region is finally written, Michael Lawson's name will clearly stand out as an important influence on the development of contemporary Seattle art.

**John Olbrantz**
*Deputy Director*
*Whatcom Museum of History and Art*

*Red Chair*, 1967
Acrylic on Masonite, 67½ by 48½ in.
Bellevue Art Museum,
Bellevue, Washington, 75.13

# MICHAEL LAWSON

## An Englishman Abroad

From the moment he set foot on American soil, the British painter Michael Lawson had found his subject: American people and their buildings, freeways, and way of life, one that, in August 1966, appeared perhaps freer and more open to possibilities than life in England. Although he lived in Seattle only from August 1967 until December 1969, Lawson left a lasting impact on Seattle art still felt today. An artist's artist, he became the city's most influential figurative painter of the 1970–1985 period. When his first museum show in the United States closed on August 6, 1972, at the University of Washington Henry Art Gallery, the machinery was set in motion for a career-in-absentia, a legend, a reputation of equal parts fact and lore, anecdote and memory.

Now a resident in his native Liverpool, Lawson continues to exhibit and paint for an admiring English public and critics. To understand his art, however, one must look at two countries—England and America—and two cities—Liverpool and Seattle. This is not a tale of two cities but a story of an Englishman abroad, an artist who found his true voice and vision in a land ripe for affection, dissection, satire, and the enthusiasm and horror of the outsider.

Born to Barbara and Charles Lawson in Liverpool on February 12, 1944, Michael Edwin Lawson was a child prodigy of sorts, spending hours painting and drawing, later pouring over issues of *Punch*, the humor magazine, and becoming absorbed in newspaper editorial cartoons. A naturally gifted cartoonist and mimic, when he entered the Liverpool College of Art in 1960 and later attended London's Royal College of Art, his early style had already developed: figurative, moody, with a faint humor emerging from difficult or desperate situations.

Unlike his L.C.A. classmate future Beatle John Lennon, Lawson spent no time strumming a guitar in hallways outside the art studio classrooms. Instead he was hardworking, prolific, amiable, and, as always, mesmerized by the human comedy about him. He studied painting and excelled in printmaking and drawing.

A scholarship in printmaking to the Royal College of Art, one of England's most prestigious art schools, allowed him to explore an extraordinary range of techniques: zinc and steel etching, aquatint, lithography, and linocuts. He often combined aspects of landscape and figuration within a single image (*Shrubbed!*, 1965). This animated reality of inanimate things, manmade or natural, would permeate all his work in the years to come, creating what painter Andrew Keating called Lawson's "living objects."[1]

London was the right place for the young northerner in 1965: Carnaby Street, Kings Road, Abbey Road, the new music he had first heard at the Cavern in Liverpool, and the pervasive youth culture that fed the artist's unceasing imagination. His continued perusal of newspapers and magazines led to a series of politically inspired collages which treated American themes (*Imperial Wizard*, 1964) before he had ever traveled to the New World.

An avid reader, Lawson also effortlessly acquired an English literary education. Along with all the greatest English artists (William Blake, J.M.W. Turner, William Hogarth, Thomas Rowlandson, Stanley Spencer, David Hockney), the influence of narrative came to deeply characterize his choice of subject matter as well as his attitude toward a painting's raison d'etre. Add to that the impact of daily tabloid newspaper editorial cartoonists like Vicky, who drew hundreds of satirical sketches of

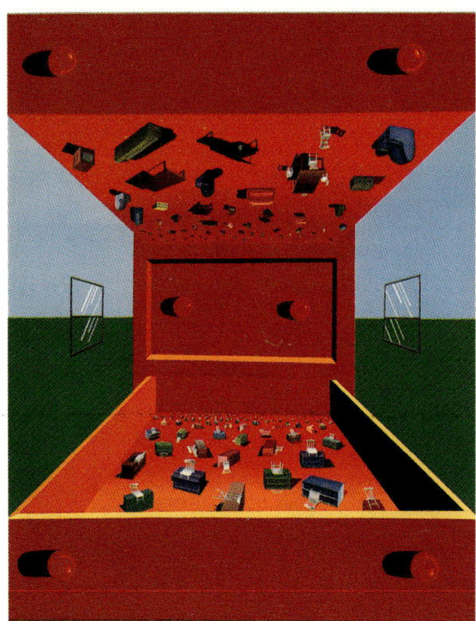

*Second Dresser*, 1966
**Enamel on Masonite, 62 by 48¾ in.**
**Lucy and Herbert Pruzan collection,**
**Seattle**
PHOTO: RICHARD NICOL

FIGURE 1

**Michael Lawson in the University District,**
**Seattle, 1969**

political figures in the late 1950s and early 1960s for the London *Evening Standard*. As a result, Lawson's figures, his comic or dramatic characters, did not really grow out of his life drawing classes. Instead they were rooted in a hybrid culture of skeptical working-class humor and a refined, impeccable sense of academic composition. This mixture of chaos and control is a pervasive theme in both the subject and execution of his art.

Lawson's next formative environment was the United States: specifically, a brief stay as a graduate fellow at the University of Wisconsin in Madison, followed by a longer, more important sojourn at the Graduate School of Art at the University of Washington. It was during Lawson's years in Madison and Seattle (1966–69) that his mature style emerged and flowered, and some of his greatest paintings were completed.

Admiring teachers such as Alistair Grant and Edwin Ladell at the R.C.A. had arranged the teaching fellowship at Madison. While there, Lawson studied with abstract painter Milton Resnick (b. 1917) and took courses in printmaking, painting, and art history. He taught basic drawing at first, and then worked as an installation assistant at the university art museum.

While at Madison, Lawson met Seattle artist Dale Chihuly, who ultimately was responsible for bringing him to the Pacific Northwest. Fellow students in the art department, Chihuly and Lawson became fast friends. Chihuly marveled at Lawson's extraordinary output, sure touch, and consuming enthusiasm for the making of art and the life of an artist: reading, drawing, painting, from dawn until late into the night.

Lawson painted his first masterpieces in Madison: *Banquet* (1966), *A Park in a Room* (1966), *Room in a Room* (1966), and *Second Dresser* (1967). Tall and flatly painted in enamels with an unusually deep perspective, they were unlike anything Chihuly had ever seen before: "This guy was the most prolific artist I ever witnessed, one of the most multitalented people, a fabulous musician and a singer and poet," Chihuly recalled. "I can only say I knew I was in the room with a genius."[2]

The Madison paintings were different from anything Lawson had done in London or Liverpool. They expressed an outsider's response to America: food overflowing a table so long it disappeared; tiny furniture tumbling out of an eerie dresser; and, in *A Park in a Room*, a weird combination of domestic interior, landscape, and nightmare. Set up like a proscenium stage complete with audience in the foreground, the picture's composition is perfectly balanced and spaced. Only upon closer inspection does something seem amiss or awry. Surrealism alone does not account for the improbable image, what Alden Mason, one of Lawson's first University of Washington professors, would call "something so disturbingly unbelievable that it couldn't be—but was."[3]

The interplay of chaos and control, hilarity and violence, impossibility and credulity, was not only an aspect of Lawson's American period, it was an aspect of what the entire country was going through in the 1960s. Stylistically, his crisp figuration, clean paint handling, and absolutely assured sense of placement were not only something his future professors at the Graduate School of Art admired enough in order to admit him. They were qualities that matched their own art. As Fay Jones (an artist Lawson met the first day he arrived in Seattle) observed, to the professors reviewing his application, Lawson's work must have looked "beyond criticism."[4]

## Before Lawson

In a dark time, the eye begins to see,
I meet my shadow
   in the deepening shade;
I hear my echo in the echoing wood—
A lord of nature weeping to a tree.

    **Theodore Roethke,
    "In a Dark Time" (ca. 1960)**

FIGURE 2

**Wendell Brazeau (1910–1974)
*Fat Jack at Ischia*, 1967
Acrylic on canvas, 28¼ by 21¾ in.
Seattle Arts Commission,
Portable Works Collection, CL84.15**

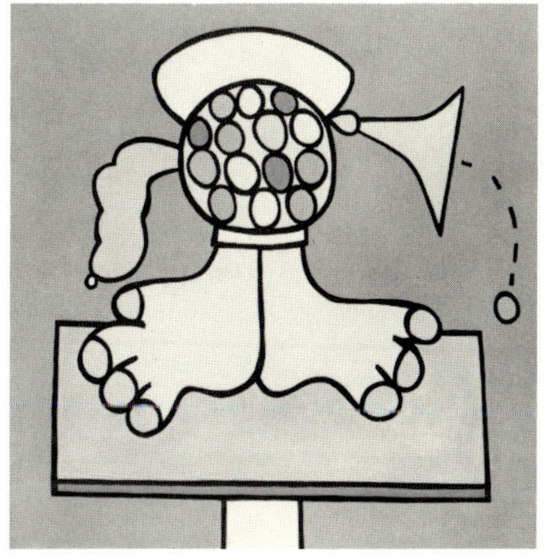

FIGURE 3

**Alden Mason (b. 1919)
*Fire One!*, 1966
Acrylic on canvas, 36 by 36 in.
Lucy and Herbert Pruzan collection, Seattle**
PHOTO: RICHARD NICHOL

*Apartment Building*, 1968
Enamel on Masonite, 67½ by 48½ in.
Peter and Debra Rettman collection, Seattle

When Lawson arrived at the University of Washington in 1967, he found a remarkably sophisticated campus with distinguished faculty members, including Pulitzer Prize–winning poet Theodore Roethke (1908–1963). Roethke's moody lyric poetry corresponded to the works of the leading members of the brooding Northwest school of art: Guy Irving Anderson (b. 1906), Kenneth Callahan (1905–1987), Morris Graves (b. 1910), and Mark Tobey (1890–1976). They had dominated the art scene off-campus since the 1950s, with Roethke as an unofficial laureate to their mystical-ecological inspirations.

On campus, however, School of Paris modernism had been institutionalized since the 1919 arrival of Australian-born post-impressionist Ambrose Patterson (1877–1966) and the 1923 appointment as dean of Walter F. Isaacs (1886–1964). Both men had exhibited extensively in Paris (Patterson with Monet, Isaacs with Picasso) before accepting their professorships, and both continued to make frequent trips abroad from the 1930s through the 1950s, keeping up ties with European friends.

A comparatively progressive curriculum was set up with a strong emphasis on still life and life drawing tempered by an open, "experimental" attitude: a tolerance for abstraction. Several former students —Frederick Anderson (1917–1993), Wendell Brazeau (1910–1974), Alden Mason (b. 1919), and Spencer Moseley (b. 1925)—became fellow faculty members after World War II in order to accommodate increased enrollment due to returning ex-G.I.s.

Moseley and Brazeau had each spent a crucial year in Paris at Fernand Léger's private atelier, and their own brand of Léger's "tubism" (a controlled figurative formalism using a limited, usually primary, palette) was already highly devel-

oped. The climate of a cool abstraction went farther as other teachers with similar sensibilities were added by Isaacs and his successor, Boyer Gonzales (1909–1987).

Encouraged by Chihuly to come to Seattle, Lawson applied and was accepted at the University of Washington with a research assistantship in 1967. Before he arrived, Mason and other faculty members marveled at the works he submitted for entrance. "He's got it," Mason remembers commenting at the time, sharing the unanimous enthusiasm of the admissions committee. "This was the perfect place of all art schools in America for Michael to come to."

Yes and no. While it is futile to hypothesize what might have happened had Lawson gone elsewhere or, indeed, returned to England after Madison, his sojourn in Seattle carried a high personal price. Although resulting in some of the greatest paintings he ever created, it also saw the breakup of his marriage to Dorothy Smith; a tumble into madness, an attempted suicide, and hospitalization; and the severing of his American period with his abrupt flight home in 1969. But all that, the ecstasy and the terror, was ahead of Lawson as he and Chihuly drove west into the night in the summer of 1967.

### Summer of Love

I have to admit
    it's getting better,
getting better all the time
    (it can't get no worse) . . .

**The Beatles,
"Getting Better" (1967)**

When Lawson and Chihuly arrived in Seattle, the battles between the Establishment and the baby-boom generation were not yet pitched. It was the Summer

**Woman I, 1969**
**Acrylic on Masonite, 48 by 48 in.**
**Private collection, Tacoma**
PHOTO: TERRY RISHEL

to be crushed by a tumbling brick wall marked "Democratic Party." In another cartoon, LBJ, wearing a gladiator helmet, sprays gasoline on a wall of flames marked "Vietnam" and exclaims, "Jes' can't seem to put this fire out!"

Three Feiffer-like multipanel cartoons, "The Cynic," "The Director of Traffic," and "The Students," show a more critical side of Lawson usually concealed in his funny, brightly colored paintings. In "The Director of Traffic" a man in uniform is interviewed on a mock television program, "The World As It Is."

Taking the form of a dialogue, the cartoon also points up Lawson's gift for theatrical dialogue which, in turn, underscores how the figures in his paintings may function as characters in a play, something painter Gene Gentry McMahon summed up: "He has the tragic view of life that's also comic— like English theater."[7]

Like a ten-minute playlet listening in on an Orwellian comedy, "The Director of Traffic" concludes with an absurd explanation of his predecessor's dismissal: "He was relieved of his position, eventu-

***Woman III,* 1969**
**Enamel on Masonite, 48 by 48 in.**
**Marjan and Ron Petty collection, Seattle**
PHOTO: CHRISTOPHER DAHL

cially the *Helix* cartoons, was rooted in observable reality. They reinforce the written-word roots of Lawson's narrative paintings and remind us how extreme social satire in Britain is often closely tied to the anti-Establishment theater and tabloid press. In *Helix*, Lawson shifted his attitude from appreciative outsider to knowing insider, pointing out what was wrong with American culture: the war in Vietnam, student apathy, and an increasing paranoia of official oversight into peoples' lives. (Indeed, when Lawson attempted suicide and was institutionalized at Western State Hospital in Steilacoom, his cartoons would take on a prophetic character.)

For example, in "Curtain Call for the Power Structure," President Lyndon Johnson is master of ceremonies before a descending curtain of dollar bills decorated above with vignettes of African Americans caught in a burning ghetto; National Guard troops presided over by Chicago Mayor Richard Daley; a nude Richard Nixon being scrubbed clean by cherubs; and, hovering above Johnson, Vice-President Hubert Humphrey about of Love, the high point of the blissful hippie era on the West Coast. Not until the following summer would violence begin to override the fun, both for America, and, in a way, for Lawson: Robert Kennedy's assassination; the Chicago riots at the Democratic presidential convention; the run for the presidency by racist candidate George Wallace; the bombing of R.O.T.C. headquarters on the U.W. campus; protest marches against the war in Vietnam.

Lawson's stay in Seattle would be split in two: from Summer of Love to Days of Rage, from joy to madness, from outsider to insider, from graduate student to a kind of Gulley Jimson status for the Seattle art scene, recalling the character in Joyce Cary's 1944 novel *The Horse's Mouth.* The three-year period would become a marriage of heaven and hell. But the extraordinary fact of Lawson's life has been his artistic production, his acute imaginative power, and a continued immersion in his art despite personal setbacks and ill health. He responded to the hedonism and lavish overconsumption of American society in a series of enamel-on-Masonite paintings that are perhaps his greatest works.

Fay Jones remembers meeting Lawson at a picnic on the day he arrived from Wisconsin, shortly before the autumn academic term began. Later, once the steady stream of paintings began, she noted that his style of zany figuration was already "in the wind. Like [San Francisco artist John] Altoon, that sort of cartoony thing. But I liked the flatness of Lawson's color, those acid yellows and greens."

Paintings like *Red Chair* (1967), *Running Furniture* (1967), and *Untitled* (1967) were all executed during that first academic year. Lawson was very happy to be in Seattle, which reminded him of Liverpool, another port town. And despite Professor Mason's memories of how he and his colleagues aided the new foreign student—"We helped him to organize his direction, to use flatter and brighter color instead of trying to  pattern every area,"—Lawson claims, "I knew what I wanted to do and I appreciated Fred and Alden, but there were others who wanted to put their two penneth in."[5]

If there was a kindred spirit on the faculty, it was Frederick Anderson, whom Lawson says he "tended to get along with; he was such an amenable guy." Mason agrees, and goes farther: "Fred had a lot to do with [Lawson's] keeping on in the comic strip vein. The cartoon narrative—we told him it was wonderful but Fred suggested if [he] could simplify things, they would be stronger." Examples of Anderson's own much earlier art (i.e., *The City*, 1947) had expressed an ominous and hallucinatory quality comparable to Lawson's apartment building paintings, complete with gridded windows and see-through floor plans.

According to Jones, Lawson's relationship to the U.W. faculty was reciprocal: "Both Alden and Fred had that humorous side already but Lawson gave [Anderson] the courage to do figurative art again. . . . He reminded them all [Anderson, Brazeau, Mason, Moseley] of the freedom you have to do whatever you want."

Working day and night, writing, painting, and playing music, Lawson also found time to make many new friends, including sculptor Ron Petty and painter Alfredo Arreguin, and to observe pub life at off-campus hangouts. In addition, he contributed cartoons to the alternative newspaper of the day, *Helix.* According to editor Paul Dorpat, Lawson simply would walk into the *Helix* office and hand him cartoons which had a "Jules Feiffer quality."[6]

Even though Lawson's paintings seem the wildest flights of fancy, his work, espe-

*Department Store*, 1969
Enamel on Masonite, 47 by 72 in.
Private collection, Seattle
PHOTO: RICHARD NICOL

*Running Furniture*, 1967
Enamel on Masonite, 48 by 65 in.
Dale Chihuly collection, Seattle
PHOTO: TERRY RISHEL

*Two Women,* 1969
**Acrylic on Masonite, 48 by 48 in.**
**Bill and Gene McMahon collection, Seattle**
PHOTO: CHRISTOPHER DAHL

ally, when he had a freeway built on wheels and started directing it in a direction opposite to the cars that were on it. Consequently, everything stayed in the same place."[8]

In a 1967 article in *Northwest Today* magazine, a Sunday supplement to the *Seattle Post-Intelligencer,* Tom Robbins compared Lawson's art with a popular but controversial play of the period, *Tiny Alice* (1964), by Edward Albee. The play's set contains a model of the mansion occupied by the actors, who gradually realize it is more than a replica. Whatever happens to the dollhouse happens to the set, including a fire in one wing.

This curious reversal of scale and its disastrous consequences, key motifs in Lawson's art, are seen in his most concentrated and violent painting ever, *Untitled Triptych* (1967). The work was influenced by a week Lawson spent alone in New York City; one of the panels was completed there. It deals with "part of the terror of being in New York" and, indeed, expresses vividly what Lawson called "imminent danger. It is a series of observed situations that could never exist

**Woman II, 1969**
**Acrylic on Masonite, 48 by 48 in.**
**Dale Chihuly collection, Seattle**
PHOTO: CHRISTOPHER DAHL

in reality."

An outgrowth of Lawson's small notebook paintings, the triptych shows three abstracted, cutaway views of apartment buildings à la Fred Anderson. Each scene contains some awesome, private violence: sexual bondage, voyeurism, sadism, bestiality, immurement, cruelty to animals, murder, eating disorders, exhibitionism, suicide, and the revelation of Jesus Christ. Adolf Hitler exposes himself before a window while giving the Nazi salute. Connecting all three panels is a freeway covered not with cars but with people attached to wheels. Presented in comic-strip format with a deceptively simple palette suitable for illustration, the triptych discloses a shockingly cynical view of a private world. The terror of Lawson's style and part of his genius lie in the mix of an accessible style with such internalized horror and fear. As such, it is a watershed painting. From here on, Anderson's and Mason's advice to keep the cartoon format but simplify color and play down pattern would take hold.

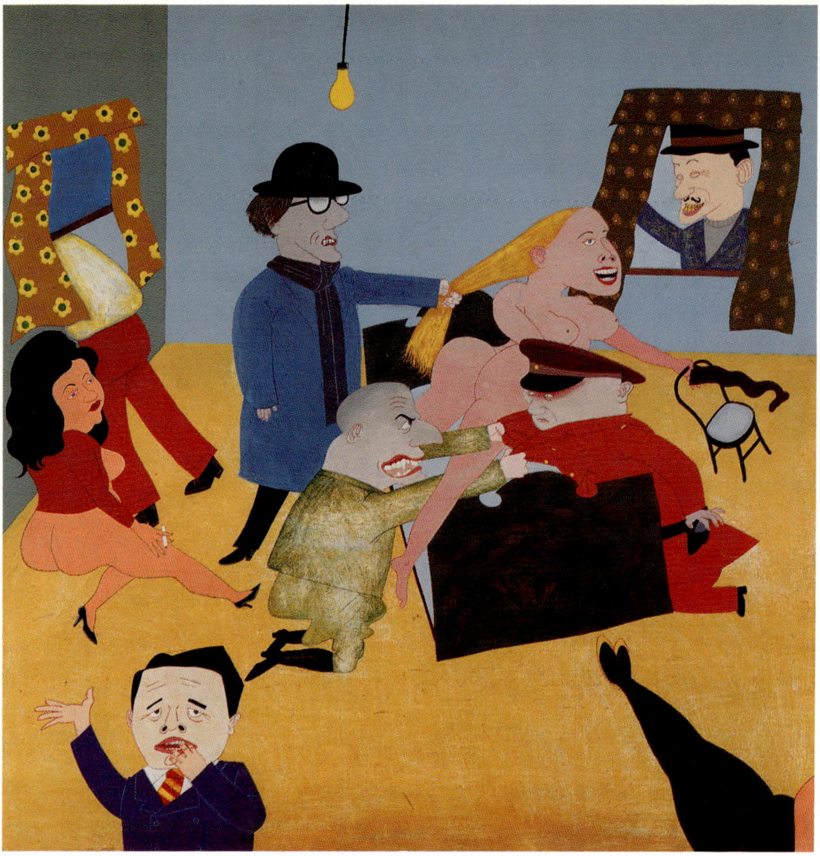

***Unknown Bed Story,* 1969**
**Acrylic on Masonite, 48 by 48 in.**
**Patti Warashina and Robert Sperry collection, Seattle**
PHOTO: TERRY RISHEL

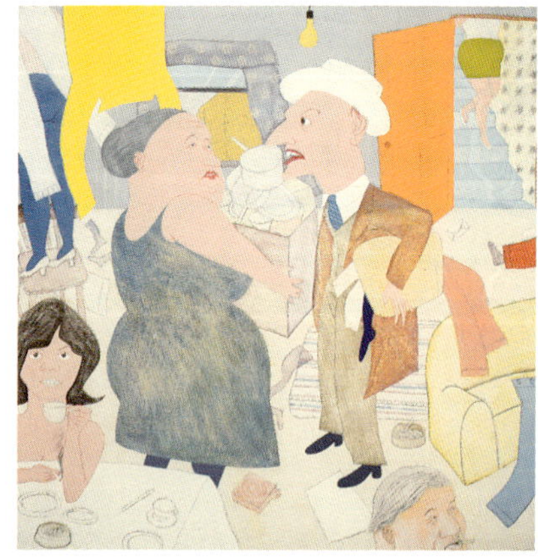

***Annie's Living-Breakfast Room,* 1969**
**Acrylic on Masonite, 48 by 48 in.**
**Dale Chihuly collection, Seattle**
PHOTO: CHRISTOPHER DAHL

## The Age of Lawson

Nineteen-sixty-nine was a prolific, epochal year for Lawson. He completed major enamel works like *Department Store* and in mid-year shifted to acrylic which, in turn, led to a different kind of surface—pale pastels and almost sanded-down areas—and a different kind of image: single figures against solid-color backgrounds (*Women I–III, Two Women*).

*Department Store* continues the improbable scale reversals (a salesman single-handedly lifts an automobile; an elephant occupies a changing room behind a curtain), but its narrative is less dependent upon the comic strip box. Figures move in and out of space but that space suggests several floors seen at once. As Mason noted: "The yellow floor was close to the smaller [areas] and then, bang! it's still like a comic strip. It walks one back into space, those areas march [one] back."

The half-dozen acrylic paintings of women, alone or in pairs, dressed in contemporary fashions (pedal pushers, mini-skirts), convey the individualized identities of each figure, although none is a strict portrait. These Masonite panels epitomize Lawson's departure from complicated, crammed compositions toward better balanced and simplified presentations.

By the time of Lawson's exhibition at the Henry Art Gallery in the summer of 1972, the artist was long gone. During a brief, unsuccessful teaching stint at Cornish College of the Arts in Seattle, he had joined a charismatic Episcopalian sect at St. Luke's Church in the Ballard neighborhood. His wife, Dorothy Smith, had left him for a philosophy professor who had befriended them both. At the same time, Lawson's grip on reality was gradually deserting him, making it difficult to function on an everyday basis. After a brief hospitalization following a suicide attempt, he returned to England, where he has lived ever since.

**FIGURE 4**

**Andrew Keating (b. 1948)**
***INSTITUSHUN***, 1975
**Acrylic on canvas, 56 by 72 in.**
**Collection of the artist, Brooklyn**
PHOTO: RON STEINBERG

**FIGURE 5**

**Gene Gentry McMahon (b. 1942)**
***No Muscle Beach***, 1982
**Oil on canvas, 45½ by 80½ in.**
**Washington State Ferries collection**
PHOTO: DIRK PARK

**FIGURE 6**

**Linda Beaumont (b. 1950)**
***I'll Meet You in the Wallroom***, 1976
**Gouache on paper, 17¾ by 25¾ in.**
**Patti Warashina and Robert Sperry collection, Seattle**

New students at the Graduate School of Art heard about Lawson via myth and anecdote; some would have seen the Henry Art Gallery exhibition. Various aspects of his art began to have their effect on the next generation of figurative painters who came in contact with his work. His former teachers borrowed what they found useful, too.

For Gene Gentry McMahon (b. 1942), it was the double-edged humor: funny and scary. Formal elements like composition made an impression, too: "There's something about the way he combined the figure and architectural elements, the poetry between those elements, they relate so beautifully."

Andrew Keating (b. 1948) admires the mixture of figuration and formalism in Lawson's work but adds "the element of psychosis." Keating was attracted to the alienation of Lawson's figures, a theme he feels dominated Cold War culture. The extremism of subject matter, Keating comments, was validated by the comparably obsessive nature of the picture's finish in enamel or acrylic. Lawson's characters were "constrained and sweating," coexisting with the animated furniture Keating calls "living objects."

For Keating's own art, Lawson reinforced a personal expression of anguish but with the younger artist's concomitant confessional content influenced by feminist art of the 1970s. The flat areas of color, claustrophobic interiors, and seething unease also had an evident impact on Keating.

"Going into the Henry Art Gallery show was pivotal for me, like Alice in Wonderland," Linda Beaumont (b. 1950) reminisced: "I can remember at that age [twenty-one], it just opened me to what painting could be. It was lysergic, pow! . . . Against the background of the boy's club at the painting department, Lawson gave me permission to combine image and symbol." [9] Building on Lawson's example, Beaumont simplified and compressed her images yet retained a threatening uncertainty still present in her work today. Sharing Mason's admiration for multilevel space, she felt she "could just travel in those paintings and stay there."

As to the sources of some of the recurring images in Lawson's work, Beaumont observes: "He just played here for a while; he laughed at Seattle but he created a story with no beginning, middle, or end, and a composition with a determined warping of scale and figure."

Thus influenced by Lawson, McMahon, Keating, and Beaumont went on to become some of the most important figurative painters in Seattle during the 1970–1985 period. They extended the campus taste for formalist figuration begun by Anderson, Mason, Moseley, and Brazeau which would, in time, be further reinforced by the arrival of Jacob Lawrence in 1970.

These artists, all strong individuals yet sharing the qualities mentioned above—alienation, flat areas of color, zany humor, balanced composition—might find themselves joined in a belatedly titled era, the Age of Lawson. Different from the Chicago Hairy Who with their deeper debt to Surrealism, separate from funk art in northern California with its love of puns and scatological slant, the Age of Lawson artists stressed humor in the face of extremity, unblended and pure color, balanced yet complicated composition, and a spectrum of social and private subjects with an emphasis on the plight of the individual.

## Return to Liverpool

I get by with a little help
    from my friends,
gonna try with a little help
    from my friends.

**The Beatles,
"With a Little Help from My Friends" (1967)**

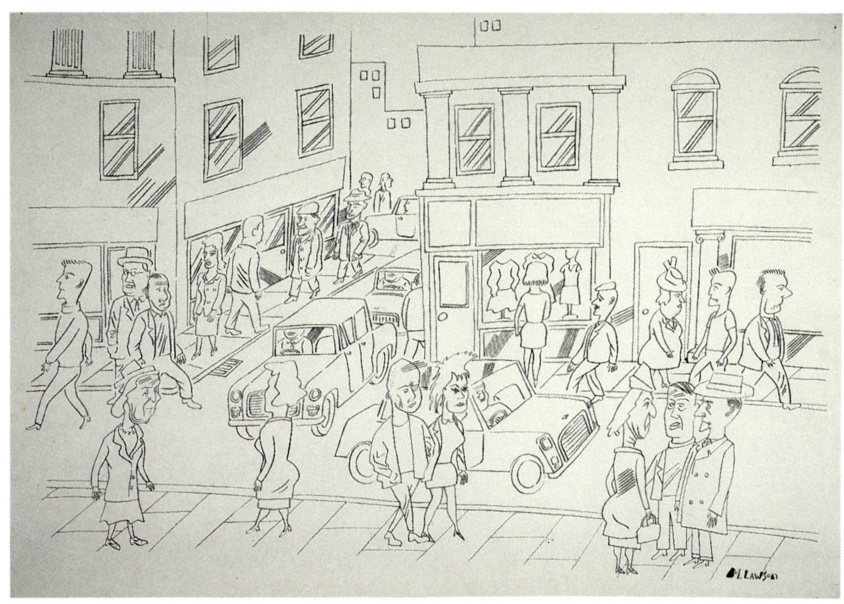

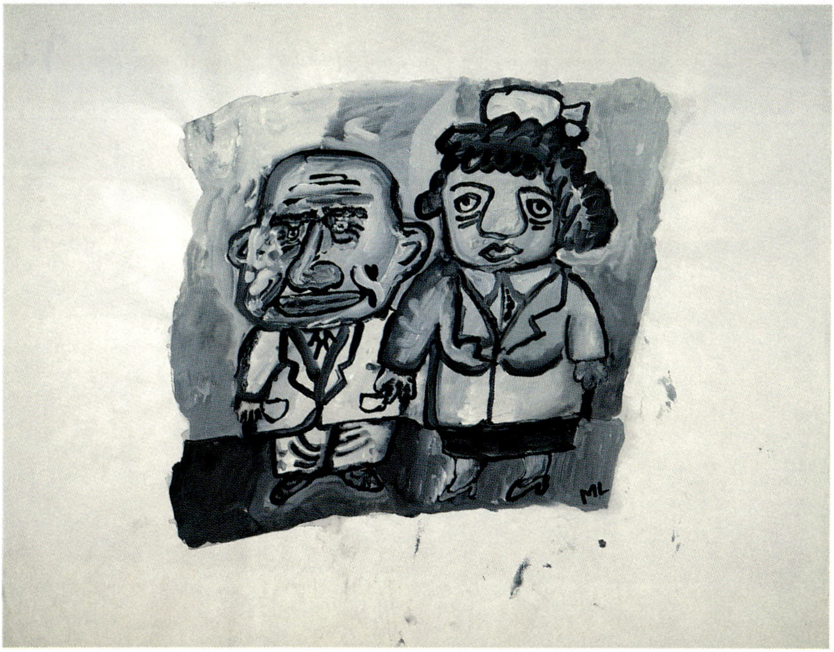

FIGURE 7

**Michael Lawson**
***The Street,* 1985**
**Ink on paper, 21½ by 31½ in.**
**Dale Chihuly collection, Seattle**
PHOTO: TERRY RISHEL

FIGURE 8

**Michael Lawson**
***Doctor and a Nurse,* 1985**
**Ink on paper, 15 by 20 in.**
**Private collection, Tacoma**
PHOTO: TERRY RISHEL

*Card Players*, 1985
Oil on Masonite, 60 by 48 in.
Dale Chihuly collection, Seattle
PHOTO: CHRISTOPHER DAHL

The twenty years after Lawson's Seattle period have been marked by ups and downs. As Lawson put it: "The 1960s were very bright with hope. The 1970s were a decade of purgatory. The 1980s were a period of recovery, and the 1990s are a period of stabilization. My past is being restored to me."

Despite hospitalizations for manic-depressive illness, Lawson still paints and draws. He shifted to oils in 1979, and with the support of his parents, with whom he lived until their deaths (in 1979 and 1993), Lawson has continued to produce drawings and notebook paintings when unable to undertake large-scale works.

In works created in the early 1970s, Lawson maintained the crisp execution he had perfected in America. *Grocery Store* (1972), *Abrahams and Isaacs* (1972), *Bus Queue* (1973), and *Railway Carriage* (1973) are sympathetic and witty observations of Liverpool's street life. These were joined by sketches (*Punks, Pubs, and Cafes*, 1982; *The Street*, 1985). Perhaps reflecting the effect of hospitalizations between 1969 and 1975, Lawson's style turned brushier, less defined, and more expressionistic. His subjects sunk into dejected and panicked situations. Religious scenes, including illustrations of John Bunyan's novel, *Pilgrim's Progress* (1973); *Scenes from the Life of Christ* (1973–74), and *The Temptations of St. Anthony* (1978), grew out of the artist's renewed commitment to evangelical Christianity.

Gone was the sun-filled zaniness of the Seattle years, replaced with a more mature, seasoned and melancholy sensibility. Instead of policemen gone amok and runaway furniture, Lawson depicted other personal catastrophes like *Jonah and the Whale* (ca. 1985) and *The Rapturing* (ca. 1983), an El Greco–like vision of the Second Coming.

Lawson returned to Seattle in 1986, when many of the later paintings were

FIGURE 9

**Michael Lawson**
*Club Scene 2*, 1985
**Ink on paper, 16½ by 11¾ in.**
**Private collection, Seattle**
PHOTO: TERRY RISHEL

FIGURE 10

**Michael Lawson**
*Pub Scene*, 1985
**Ink on paper, 16 by 20 in.**
**Dale Chihuly collection, Seattle**
PHOTO: TERRY RISHEL

FIGURE 11

**Harold Gilman (1876–1919)**
***Mrs. Mounter,* ca. 1916**
**Oil on canvas, 36⅛ x 24¼ in.**
**Copyright © Trustees of the**
**National Museums and**
**Galleries on Merseyside,**
**Walker Art Gallery,**
**Liverpool, 3135**

shown at the Gordon Woodside/John Braseth Gallery. Besides revisiting Chihuly and old friends like Arreguin and Petty, Lawson saw his American paintings for the first time in seventeen years. He commented: "I was knocked out. They could have been done by a total stranger." All the same, the three-week Seattle stay "influenced me for the next five years." The Woodside exhibit displayed nearly a dozen paintings including the Cézannesque *Card Players* (1985). In a narrow palette recalling the French painter, Lawson developed his own churning, agitated brushwork, which, pushed against the resistant Masonite support, much more explicitly communicates a sense of an emotionally charged space than the flat and cool American works.

Many of the later drawings are set in pubs or discos and, with their increasing combination of thin and shaded line, suggest German Expressionist artists like Max Beckmann and George Grosz. These similarities have been noted by Lawson's British critics, too.[10] This gradual darkening of mood and color reunites Lawson to his European roots, building on his youthful affinity to British satirists like Hogarth but veering closer to a northern European tradition of religious art and social commentary. Lawson has matured, evolved, and deepened his talents since leaving Seattle.

In a poem written on the back of one of his drawings shown in his next Seattle

**Seated Woman, ca. 1985**
**Pastel on paper, 23½ by 16½ in.**
**Dale Chihuly collection, Seattle**


exhibition at Garner/Demombynes in 1988, Lawson expressed both his powers of social observation and his conviction that we will all be subject to an imminent divine judgment: "The table / where the dancing, prancing / mad dance goes to the / tune of a frenzied time / which keeps the jig / in perpetual perpetual / activity spiralling to the final final end / in complete collapse / and oblivion / and other darkness / when justice shall / be established / and the enemy finally ousted." [11]

Few critics in Seattle foresaw the serious shift of Lawson's later English work. Looking back at the Seattle years, however, art critic-turned-novelist Tom Robbins remembered the "deep, dark psychological overtones" and the "completely genuine and wise innocence" of Lawson's art. [12] Those qualities of psychological depth and an informed innocence characterize late-period Lawson and add a bass note to the wicked frivolity of the 1960s paintings. Without ever becoming a zealot or mystic, Lawson nevertheless has developed into a painter of even greater sympathy for the battered human condition with all its private hells and public foibles.

With recent works abstracting the human head into blunt visages that stare out at the viewer, the artist pushes forward into a new body of work again using bright color. He also calls back to England's "kitchen sink" realist heritage, like Harold Gilman's *Mrs. Mounter* (ca. 1916), a portrait Lawson has looked at in the Walker

*Untitled,* 1993
**Mixed media on paper,**
**11 by 8½ in.**
**Courtesy of the artist, Liverpool**
PHOTO: TERRY RISHEL

28

Art Gallery in Liverpool since he was a
child. The sad eyes, without a trace of
self-pity, stare out at the viewer in that
painting, and in Lawson's *Seated Woman*
(ca. 1985), as well as in a group of untitled
1993 mixed-media paintings on paper.

Ever evolving, constantly working, and
fully engaged in the mess of post-Thatcher
England, Michael Lawson resists easy
categorization, as all great originals do.
He had an impact on an art scene six
thousand miles away, and his Merseyside
accomplishments are gaining great respect.
Only forty-nine, his greatest paintings and
drawings still lie ahead, sure to come
before the Judgment Day.


**Notes**

1. This and subsequent comments by Andrew Keating are drawn from a conversation with the author, October 11, 1993.
2. Dale Chihuly, conversation with the author, November 8, 1993.
3. This and subsequent comments by Alden Mason are drawn from a conversation with the author, November 5, 1993.
4. This and subsequent comments by Fay Jones are drawn from a conversation with the author, November 5, 1993.
5. This and subsequent comments by Michael Lawson are drawn from a telephone conversation with the author, October 30, 1993.
6. Paul Dorpat, conversation with the author, November 11, 1993.
7. This and subsequent comments by Gene Gentry McMahon are drawn from a telephone conversation with the author, November 6, 1993.
8. *Helix*, October 10, 1968.
9. Linda Beaumont, conversation with the author, October 19, 1993.
10. Adrian Henri, "Artist at His Best," *Daily Post*, [Liverpool], April 10, 1993.
11. Michael Lawson, "The Table," unpublished poem, ca. 1985.
12. Tom Robbins, telephone conversation with the author, November 17, 1993.

## Exhibition and Collection History

Michael Lawson
Born February 12, 1944, Liverpool, England

### Education and Academic Experience

1967–68  Research Assistantship, School of Art, University of Washington, Seattle
         Instructor, Cornish College of the Arts, Seattle
1966–67  Teaching Assistantship, University of Wisconsin, Madison
1963–66  Royal College of Art, London; awarded degree, A.R.C.A., in printmaking
1960–63  Liverpool College of Art

### Selected Solo Exhibitions

1993     "Michael Lawson: The Seattle Years,"
         Whatcom Museum of History and Art, Bellingham, Washington
         Orrell Arts Centre, Liverpool
         Kathy Kaperick Gallery, Tacoma, Washington
1988     "Michael Lawson: Major Drawings/Four Paintings,"
         Garner/Demombynes Gallery, Seattle
1987     "Michael Lawson: Work From the '70s,"
         Liverpool Academy of Arts Gallery
1986     "The Return of Michael Lawson,"
         Gordon Woodside/John Braseth Gallery, Seattle
1983     Atkinson Gallery, Southport, Lancashire
1982     Bluecoat Gallery, Liverpool
1981     Picturegallery, London
1980     Murdoch Lothian Gallery, Liverpool
1979     Liverpool Academy of Arts Gallery (also 1975, 1974)
1972     Henry Art Gallery, University of Washington, Seattle
1970     Chameleon Gallery, Liverpool
1969     Gordon Woodside Gallery, Seattle (also 1968)

### Selected Group Exhibitions

1989     "Marie Curie Exhibition," Albert Dock, Liverpool
         Liverpool Academy of Arts Gallery
1988     Acorn Gallery, Liverpool (also 1987, 1986, 1984)
         "School of Art 1960–1975; 1975–1988: School of Art—University of
         Washington," SAFECO Gallery, Seattle
1987     "Branching Out," Bluecoat Gallery, Liverpool
         "Merseyside Artists," Walker Art Gallery, Liverpool (also 1983, 1985)
1986     "Small Works," Bluecoat Gallery, Liverpool
         "Eccentric Satellites," Bumbershoot Visual Arts Exhibition, Seattle Center

1985    "Bumberbiennale: Seattle Painting 1925–1985," Bumbershoot Visual Arts
        Exhibition, Seattle Center
1983    "Bumberbiennale: Art since 'Century 21,' " Bumbershoot Visual Arts
        Exhibition, Seattle Center
1977    Annual Salon, Liverpool Academy of Arts (also 1970–76)
1975    "Face of Merseyside," Walker Art Gallery, Liverpool
1969    Pacific Northwest Arts and Crafts Fair, Bellevue, Washington (also 1968)
1967    Wisconsin Salon, Madison, Wisconsin
        Milwaukee Salon, Milwaukee, Wisconsin
1966    Annual of Northwest Artists, Seattle Art Museum
        "Young Contemporaries," F.B.A. Galleries, London (also 1965, 1964)


## Public Collections

Atkinson Gallery, Southport, Lancashire
Bellevue Art Museum, Bellevue, Washington
Durham Libraries, Yorkshire
Henry Art Gallery, University of Washington, Seattle
Liverpool Royal Teaching Hospital
Pilkington Glass, Ltd., St. Helens, Lancashire
Seattle Art Museum
Seattle Arts Commission, Portable Works Collection
Tacoma Art Museum
University of Liverpool
University of Oregon Museum of Art, Eugene
Whatcom Museum of History and Art, Bellingham, Washington
Williamson Art Gallery, Birkenhead, Lancashire


## Private Collections

Alfredo Arreguin and Susan Lytle, Seattle
Diahann and John Braseth, Seattle
Dale Chihuly, Seattle
Clair Colquitt and Joyce Moty, Seattle
Robert Hamilton, London
Andrew Keating, Brooklyn, New York
Johnine Machrowicz, San Francisco
Mrs. Rose Maker, Seattle
Robert and Dee Ann Maki, Seattle
Alden Mason, Seattle
Vincent McInerny, London
Bill and Gene McMahon, Seattle
Michael and Theresa Nolan, Mercer Island, Washington
Marjan and Ron Petty, Seattle
Janine Pirion, Liverpool
Lucy and Herbert Pruzan, Seattle

Joe Reno, Seattle
Peter and Debra Rettman, Seattle
Christina Scott, Burlingame, California
Margaret Sarsfield, Liverpool
Dale Travous, Seattle
Robert Trueman, Liverpool
Patti Warashina and Robert Sperry, Seattle
William Wikstrom, Seattle
David Williams, Wallasey, Lancashire
Frank Wilson, Derby, Derbyshire
Gordon Woodside, Seattle


## Bibliography


Jean Batie, "A Hint of the Diabolic at Woodside Gallery," *Seattle Times*, February 15, 1969.

Robert Clark, "Merseyside Prints," *Guardian*, August 22, 1990.

Peter Davies, "To Those Unseen in 'Liverpool Seen,' " *Artspool*, Winter 1992.

John Entwistle, *Merseyside Artists 2*. Liverpool: Walker Art Gallery, 1985.

Regina Hackett, "A Legendary Artist Is Back with a New Style and the Same Old Edge," *Seattle Post-Intelligencer*, January 31, 1986.

———, "After 20 Years, Artist Lets His Characters Loose in a Wild World," *Seattle Post-Intelligencer*, July 1, 1988.

Adrian Henri, "Artist at His Best," *Daily Post* [Liverpool], April 10, 1993.

Matthew Kangas, *Bumberbiennale: Seattle Painting 1925–1985*. Seattle: Bumbershoot, 1985.

Matthew Kangas, "Bourgeois Claustrophobia," *Seattle Weekly*, January 29, 1986.

———, "Mike Lawson at Woodside/Braseth," *Art in America*, July 1986.

———, *School of Art 1960–1975; 1975–1988*. Seattle: SAFECO Insurance Companies, 1988.

"Lawson in Exotic Shows, Woodside . . . ," *Seattle Times*, July 18, 1972.

Stephanie Miller, "Paintings Mirror Today's Frenzied Society," *Seattle Post-Intelligencer*, July 23, 1972.

Frank Milner, "Visual Arts: Mike Lawson," *What's On* [Liverpool], January 1989.

[Tom Robbins], "Michael Lawson," *Seattle Post-Intelligencer Northwest Today*, November 5, 1967.

Christopher Schnoor, "Outside the Main Stream, Seattle, Part II," *Vision*, Fall 1986.